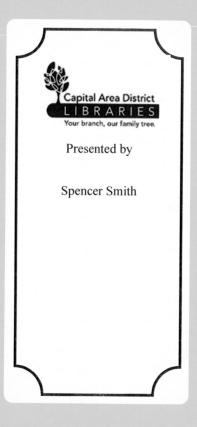

COULD YOU HUG A CACTUS?

They say "Don't judge a book by its cover." You're off to a very good start!
You've already gotten inside it and that is the very best part!

Have you seen my mate?
He's running quite late.
I've waited awhile and it's looking quite bleak.

I know he could hear.
I told him, quite clear,
"We'll start to depart at the end of next week."

COULD YOU HUG A CACTUS?

Poems by PHILLIP VAN WAGONER
Illustrations by SPENCER SMITH

Scribble Fiction

COULD YOU HUG A CACTUS?

Layout by Mike Matola
Copyediting by Naomi Long and her team at The Artful Editor
Printed in China by onthemark.net

www.scribblefiction.com

Library of Congress Control Number: 2015916111
ISBN 978-1-943568-00-0

First Edition

TO DO

Give someone a hug this morning.
Leave them with no doubt
That you like the stuff they're made of
And just what they're all about.

THE PIRATE

Black Beard got to sail the seas in search of buried treasure.
Captain Kidd embezzled gold doubloons for pride and pleasure.
Old Long Ben retired in style with spoils from picking locks.
The only loot I'm left to root is in my cereal box.

BUTTONS

Buttons is my robot.
He is seventeen feet tall.
He is stronger than a tractor.
He could walk right through a wall.

He could crush a rock to pebbles
Underneath his giant feet.
He could bowl a bigger boulder
Down the center of the street.

He could wrestle with a vessel
If battleships had arms,
Or alert the town of danger
With his thunderous alarms.

He is built with iron armor
That is dipped in liquid steel,
With a scratchless, rustless finish
And a waterproofing seal.

He has rocket boosters also!
They are built with so much power
He could fly to Rome and back to home
In under half an hour.

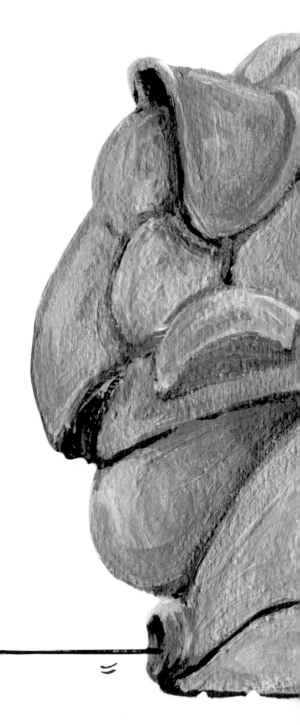

It is kind of hard to camouflage
A robot of his size
But I think you would be quite impressed
To see how hard he tries.

He's the strongest and the steadiest
Big thing you'll ever see.
While some might find him scary,
He is really good to me.

He is such an awesome robot.
He is friendly, smart, and strong,
But he's also bored;
His power cord
Is only ten feet long.

ALONE

If Grandma's in Montana
And Grandpa's in Sioux Falls
And Sweet Aunt Lil's
At Uncle Phil's,
Or was it Uncle Paul's?

If Mom is in Moldova,
And Dad went down to Dover,
Irene flew Ben
To Ireland
To find a four-leaf clover . . .

Miss Sippy headed southeast,
Miss Surry left home too.
The Hansen clan
Got in their van
And drove to Kalamazoo . . .

If everyone is elsewhere
I guess I'm out of luck.
It seems it's clear
Why no one's here
To hear me shout . . . **"I'M STUCK!!!"**

TEDDY

Teddy is a bear, you know.
A monster that can tear you so.
He'll rip through tents with fearsome paws!
(Please do not mind, they have no claws.)
You'll run and scream from one so tough!
(From seam to seam a coat of fluff.)
His fierce attacks (are soft to touch)!
The great beast roars, "I love you bear-y much!"

OUR FORT

Our fort can withstand any foe!
The Vikings and pirates won't try.
The ninjas that vowed to defeat us
Abandoned and went home to cry.

The wrestlers were wasting their time
And the elephants gave up their pushin'.
Yes, our fort is impenetrable
(As long as you don't move that cushion).

INSIDE

There lives
A man
Inside
My wall.
He does
Not have
Much room
At all.

He has
No bath,
He has
No sink.
He does
Not have
The space
To think.

He has
No couch,
He has
No chairs
Or place
To put
The clothes
He wears.

But gripes
From him
You will
Not hear,
His rent's
Two cents,
Paid once
A year!

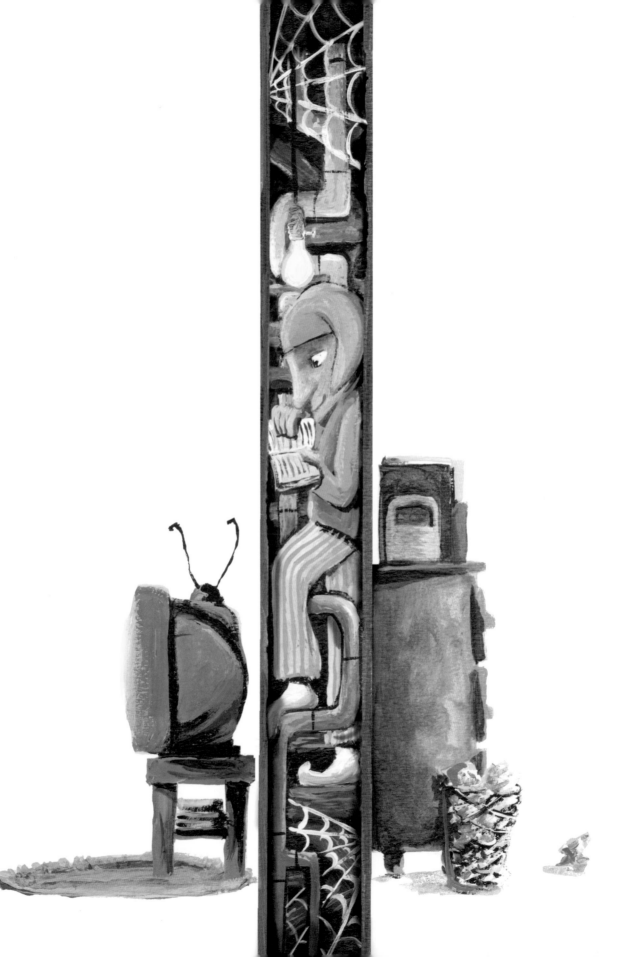

DO SOME

The books that have words: you should read 'em.
The ones that are empty: you write 'em.

The people you meet: you should friend 'em.
The battles you face: you should fight 'em.

The songs that you know: you should sing 'em.
The ones that you don't: you can hum.

You can't always do everything you want to
But you can almost always do some.

THE CLUMSY KID

It's good to be the clumsy kid
Once in every while.
Though low-hung signs are dangerous
And so are socks and tile,
And bumpy paths can lead to knees
Now bumped in the same spots,
And darkened rooms can lead to heads
All covered up in knots.
It's good to be the clumsy kid
Once in a blue moon.
I'm waiting for that time to come.
(I hope it gets here soon.)

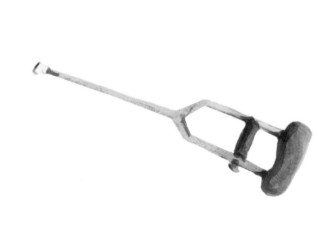

THE GROSSEST THINGS
THAT DON'T EXIST

A folispam, a tumblegrut,
Some slimy, sticky, filthy splut.
A wessel-flurp, a pibble-sneer,
A purple mucus-covered gleer.
A blechen-bleu, a garschel-snap,
A powdered bag of fattened glap.
And that is all, the complete list:
The grossest things that don't exist.

QUESTION MARK

I love my family very much,
We're close as close can be.
They tell me all about themselves,
Know everything of me.

My oldest brother, *What's-His-Name*,
Is really quite a guy.
The second oldest, *Something-Else*,
Is just a little shy.

My little sister, *Whosie-Whatsit*,
Takes care of the pets.
She walks with *Dog* and talks with *Bird*
And takes them to their vets.

My parents are a perfect pair,
Both *Dad* and charming *Mother*.
They took us on a trip to see
Our great-aunt *Some-Or-Other*.

And all the cousins were there too,
There's *Hey!* and *You!* and *Feller*,
And sweet old *Gramps* was there as well!
(He's quite the storyteller.)

He told us tales of growing up
Until the big surprise;
All his sons showed up at once
And he exclaimed, *"You Guys!"*

Later on, I didn't know
We'd packed to leave the park.
My father called me from the car, said **"Come on, '?'!!"**

I LIKE YOU

I really like it when you smile
'Cause you have the cutest dimple.
And you really like the poems I write
Even when they're really simple.

SOMETIMES IT SEEMS

Sometimes it seems unthinkable that I could lead a team
Or race a car around a track or guide a boat upstream.

Sometimes it seems I have no chance of ever fighting fires
Or saving trees or keeping bees or chasing my desires.

Sometimes it seems improbable that I could ever be
A person who is worth somebody looking up to me.

Sometimes it feels impossible that I could ever do
Anything that's great at all, until I talk to you.

COULD YOU HUG A CACTUS?

What if a cactus felt really bad?
Hurt and depressed and truly quite sad?

Feeling unwelcome or feeling unliked,
Not feeling like dealing with being all spiked.

The desert might not be a whole lot of fun.
A tumbleweed isn't much conversation.

What if it started to share all its fears?
Cry a small cry with its cactus-juice tears?

What if it gave all your heartstrings a tug?
Could you do the deed, could you give it a hug?

A FUMBLING FUNAMBULIST

Though there's a lot that we debate
(It's rare we're eye-to-eye),
There's one thing that I think you'll think
Is quite hard to deny.

Of all the folks in all the world,
(I'm sure you will agree),
A fumbling funambulist
Is an awful one to be.

TINY

There is a tiny village
In a place I can't recall.
It has a tiny clothing store
And tiny shopping mall.

It has a tiny arcade
With tiny games to play.
And many tiny houses
Along the tiny Tiny Way.

It has a tiny hair salon
And tiny grocery mart
And a tiny fire departmentIf a
tiny fire should start.

It's a perfect tiny neighborhood,
Or looks like it could be,
Except the residents of Tiny
Are as big as you and me!

PAUL THE WALRUS

Paul the Walrus stares at me.
His bulging eyes, they glare at me.
I find it all quite terribly,
Unbearably embarrassing.

You may ask me why he'd stare,
Why he has his eyes set square,
Why his unblinking ivory pair
Of peepers tells me to "Beware."

I do not think he's dumb or blind,
I understand why he's unkind
And finds me rather unrefined.
(I ate his fish when I last dined.)

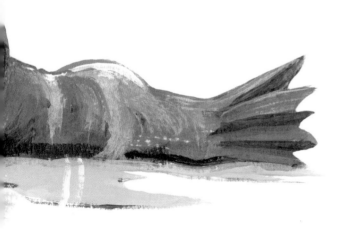

WORDS ARE WORDS

Words are words are words are real
And words can harm or words can heal
And words can hide or help reveal
The way you really truly feel.

Words are words are pretty things.
They leap from tongue when your heart sings
To match the song on your heartstrings
And share the noise of joy it brings.

Words are words are words are strong
And words can change who gets along
Or make you feel you don't belong
When words are words are words are wrong.

Words are words are bigger still
Than castles or the paper mill
For without words we could not build,
Since building plans are all word-filled.

Words are words are letters too,
Just twenty-six arranged by you.
A mixed and matched-up alphabet stew
To share the thoughts your brain can spew.

And words are words and words can play
But words can hurt in the same way.
Be careful with your words today:
There's strength in every one you say.

LEFT FIELDER

My baseball cap's too droopy.
I cannot see at all.
So I just hold my glove up
In case they hit the ball.

They keep me out in left field,
They never let me swing.
They think that I'm not able—
I just can't see a thing.

The game has gotten quiet
Since top of the last inning.
There may not be a crowd here
Or maybe we're not winning.

But Coach has always told me,
"Go out and have some fun!"
Well I've had hours of fun now,
I'm ready to be done.

My arm is getting tired,
And it's begun to rain.
I'm getting pretty hungry.
But don't mean to complain . . .

For when this game is over,
I'll see my name displayed:
"Left fielder in the longest
Baseball game ever played."

EDWARD VS. THE MANNEQUIN

"A double-jump and there, I win!"
Said Edward to the mannequin.
"I won at chess and marbles, too,
and jumping rope looked hard for you.

"You couldn't get your kite to fly.
You couldn't skip, but did you try?
And can you say you gave your all
Without one shot in basketball?

"I raced you to the tree and back—
That time I was defeated.
But isn't there a tiny chance
That possibly you cheated?

"I would have won at Battleship,
But you were too afraid.
So then I won at Go Fish! twice
And three times at Old Maid.

"I won at almost everything,
But still, I'm quite impressed.
No matter how I try and try,
You win the stare contest."

HERO

I got thin arms—long, thin arms—
How I used to loathe 'em.
For they are frail
And strange and pale And it is hard
to clothe 'em.

But recently, Sue dropped her key
And it fell down the sewer.
So I marched in with arms so thin
Now I'm a hero to 'er.

P.S.: She's cute and kind, to boot.
(I'm awful glad I found 'er.)
We've got a date at half past eight!
(I might wrap my arms around 'er.)

AN ODE TO IRON-BUTT BYNUM

There's a man from Maine,
With steel for a rear—
I didn't think I'd mind him.

But when he came by,
My chairs ran in fear,
And now I cannot find 'em.

That man is gone,
He split last week,
And left my house behind him.

But that, you see,
Is the worst place to be—
Behind Old Iron-Butt Bynum.

FOOTNOTE

I must admit I love my feet.
Their usefulness just can't be beat.
My person-props deserve a hand,
For without them, I could not stand.

I could not walk or run or jump,
And if I tried, I'd just go "thump!"
I could not skip beside the street
Without my trusty, dusty feet.

I could not climb a giant tree
Without my feet right under me.
While I'm not part of the ballet,
It's nice to know I could someday.

They are my legs' two favorite friends,
Supporting always from the ends
And smelling pepperminty too!
That's what I think, but what do you?

INDEX

ACKNOWLEDGMENTS

"Paul the Walrus" was inspired by a picture drawn by the talented Charlie Bink. The rest I just made up.

SPECIAL THANKS

Mike Matola, whose insight and assistance helped shape the book and get it made.

Naomi Long and the team at The Artful Editor for their keen eyes and knowledge of the English language.

Silvana Gargione for her generosity and invaluable advice on how to get the process started.

Dave Cain and Dunbar Dicks for your help in getting our message out to the world.

Phillip would like to thank Kelly, Mom & Dad, Patrick, and Mike Azzopardi for encouraging all of these ideas.

Spencer would also like to thank Mom, Dad, Grandma Claire, Jim, Grant and Ely for their never-ending support.

The finest of the finer folks, these amazing people helped make the book real. Thank you!

Jackson Thomas, David Lawson, Madeleine Kudritzki and Jeff Berg, The Incredible Mulk, Mike Azzopardi, Dave Cain, Allyson Rees and Julius Metoyer III, Malcolm Pierce Myers, Peggy Van Wagoner, Laura Moran, Leah Karagosian, Michael and Nancie Freeborn, Rowena Roque, Erika Barczak, Alex Talsma, Louis Balestra Di Nolfi, Maya S., the Smiley Family, Dan Dabrowski, Beth Correll, Anna Tebben, Jeny Quine, Greg Smith, Nic and Shara Angell, Greg Richman, Colin Rich, the Filosa Family, Jackie Hakim, James and Luke Caralis, Jimmy Smith, Felix Johnstone, Hank and Rosalie Harper, Suzanne Engle, Alex Lyle, Christine Maffucci, Rob and Erin Walker, C. Boutain, Ami Hirsh, Crystal Miles, Chad Swan-Badgero, Andrew and Sarah Dobos, Lissette Schettini, Patricia Smith, Rae Hogan, Kiel Gookin and Robin Reader, Shane Spiegel, Harry Matheu, Olivia and Ben, Emily Broderdorf, Dutch Slager, Michele Azenzer Bear, Joe, Annie, Mara, Robbie, Zeke, and Lily Mueller, Rich and Ryan Cherecwich, Kim Mueller, Mike, Amity, Kade, Arden, and Mak, Melanie Crescenz, Paul VanWagoner, Lucas Hearn, Matthew and Laura McKinley, Botiki Boutique, Timothy Ryder, Kristen Creager, Kathy Roper, Nina Bargiel, Fancy and Popsy Ralston, MC Froyo-Mike, Kathryn Takis, William Edwards, Jeff Bushell, Jerry Jorgensen, Danielle Mamagona, John S Dorsey, Karen and Terry Larkin, the Visker Family, Kelly and Jennifer Johnson, Frufru Nanner, Joseph Servillo, JR Kudritzki, Frankie Sanchez, the Kenny Hogans, Ely LaMay, the Accavitti Family, Team Azzowin, Tim Hulst, Ron and Jenny Huibers, Edith May Hedges, Ann Baldree on behalf of Andrew Flowers, Richard and Kyra, MiddleBar, Amanda Farris, Jeanie Morris, Aunt Becky and Uncle Bud, Wendy Smith, Vicky Bramley, Emanuel Craciunescu, Bruce Van Wagoner (proud father), Henry and William Tagliere, Viviana Soto, Brian Nagahashi, Amanda MacFadden, Will Sampson, Eric and Amy Barron, Karen and Jerry Jennings, Angelee Krumm, Marci Hooper, Scott Oldeman, Benjamin Michael and Bradley Mitchell Newton, Erin Ochi, Gary Swiggett, Tom Humphrey, the VanDyke Family, Martha and Jerrell Hutson, Jennifer Galati, Alan Martin, Richard and Barbara Boutain, John and Mary Roberts, Larry Carlson, Mike Hebert, Casey and Lucia, CP, and everyone who supported this book on Kickstarter. We couldn't have done it without you.

Did you see my friend
On your way to the end?
For the end is the place that he said we would start.

I've been here for ages
On the last of the pages
Just waiting on him so that we can depart.